maiten

WOMEN ON THE EDGE 4

Translated by Margarita Raimundez
Language Consultants: Mila Maren and Tyrone Merriner

RIVERHEAD BOOKS
NEW YORK

THE BERKLEY PUBLISHING GROUP
Published by the Penguin Group
Penguin Group (USA) Inc.
375 Hudson Street, New York, New York 10014, USA
Penguin Group (Canada), 10 Alcorn Avenue, Toronto, Ontario M4V 3B2, Canada
(a division of Pearson Penguin Canada Inc.)
Penguin Books Ltd., 80 Strand, London WC2R 0RL, England
Penguin Group Ireland, 25 St. Stephen's Green, Dublin 2, Ireland (a division of Penguin Books Ltd.)
Penguin Group (Australia), 250 Camberwell Road, Camberwell, Victoria 3124, Australia
(a division of Pearson Australia Group Pty. Ltd.)
Penguin Books India Pvt. Ltd., 11 Community Centre, Panchsheel Park, New Delhi—110 017, India
Penguin Group (NZ), cnr Airborne and Rosedale Roads, Albany, Auckland 1310, New Zealand
(a division of Pearson New Zealand Ltd.)
Penguin Books (South Africa) (Pty.) Ltd., 24 Sturdee Avenue, Rosebank, Johannesburg 2196, South Africa

Penguin Books Ltd., Registered Offices: 80 Strand, London WC2R 0RL, England

WOMEN ON THE EDGE 4

Copyright © 1998 by Maitena Burundarena
English translation copyright © 2005 by Penguin Group (USA) Inc.
Cover design by Marta Borrell
Cover art by Maitena

All rights reserved. No part of this book may be reproduced, scanned,
or distributed in any printed or electronic form without permission.
Please do not participate in or encourage piracy of copyrighted
materials in violation of the author's rights.
Purchase only authorized editions.
RIVERHEAD is a registered trademark of Penguin Group (USA) Inc.

PRINTING HISTORY
Previously published in Spanish by Editorial Atlantida, S.A. (Argentina), 1998
First Riverhead trade paperback edition: March 2005
Riverhead trade paperback ISBN: 1-59448-096-6

This book has been catalogued with the Library of Congress.

Printed in the United States of America

10 9 8 7 6 5 4 3 2 1

maitena

WOMEN ON THE EDGE 4

741.5
MA1

Paterson Free Public Library
250 Broadway
Paterson, New Jersey 07501

TO

Verónica

Flavia

Rita

Amparito

Pepa

Sandra

Elena

María

Paula

Ximena

Elsa

Anabella

Julia

Cristine

Mila

Natasha

and Cynthia

THE REQUIRED AMOUNT OF FRIENDS FOR MY FIRST THIRTY-SIX YEARS OF LIFE

FRIENDS: YOU LOVE THEM, YOU LOVE THEM NOT

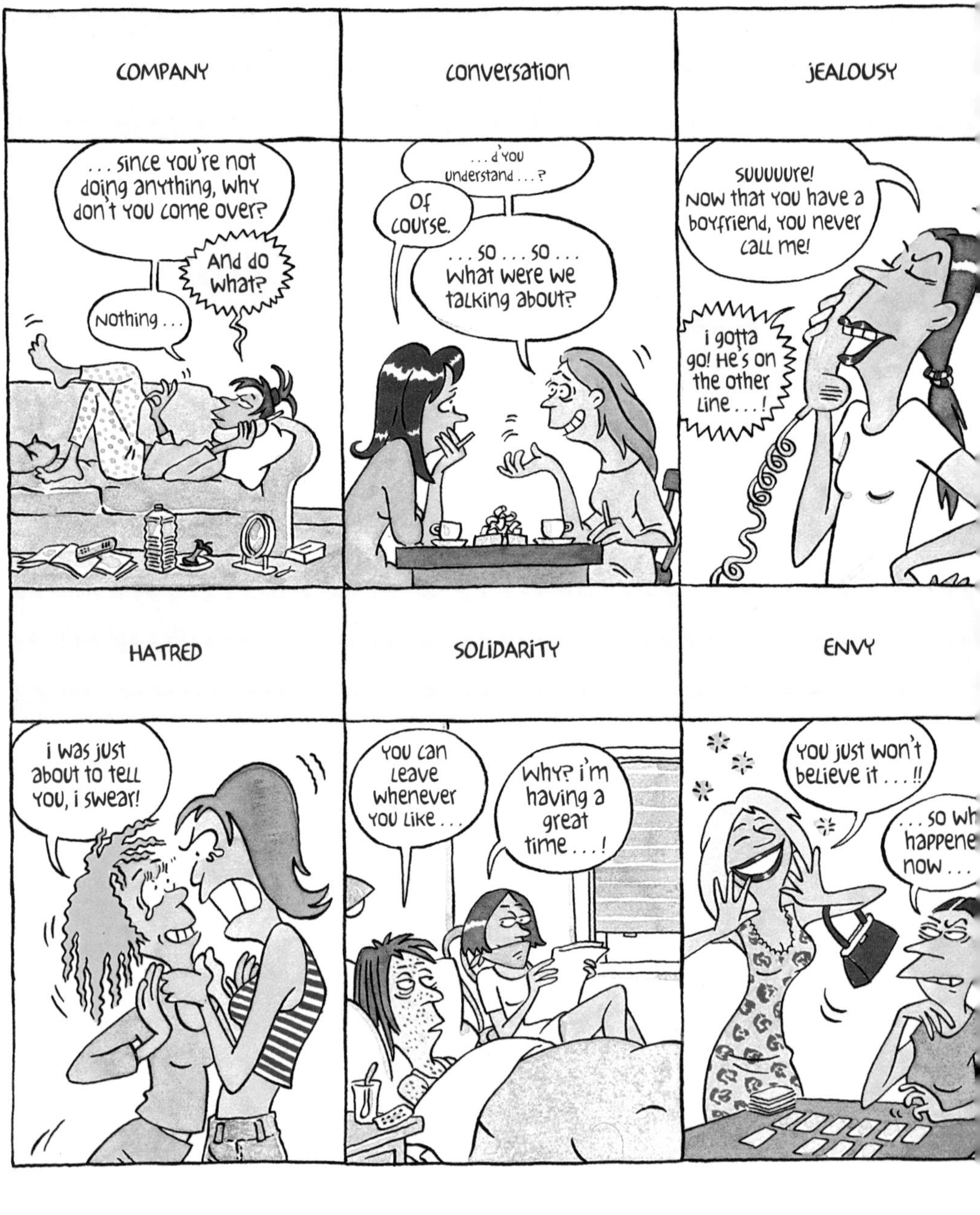

THIRTY-SOMETHING AND OTHER ANXIETY DISORDERS

THE MIND IS WILLING BUT THE FLESH IS . . . OVER THIRTY!

SIX THINGS THAT ARE HARD TO FIND

OTHER TYPES OF PENIS ENHANCERS

STANDARD OPERATING PROCEDURES

IDEAL MEN

THE WARM FUZZIES

UNCOMFORTABLE SILENCES

THE GHOST OF FASHIONS PAST

THE DEMURE BATHING COSTUMES OF THE '20S (ideal for cellulite sufferers)

THE 1900'S CORSETS (ideal for re-distributing extra pounds)

THE RUBENESQUE FLESHINESS OF ROMANTICISM (ideal for unrestricted eating, sans gym, sans guilt)

THE EVER-FLATTERING ROMAN TUNICS (ideal for disguising wide hips, large behinds, expansive bellies and/or thick ankles)

THE GLAMOROUS MYSTERY OF THE '50S SUN HATS (ideal for keeping imperfections in general, and wrinkles in particular, from the natural light)

THE BACK-TO-BASICS CAVEWOMAN LOOK (ideal cure for post-traumatic waxing disorder ... and men!)

RELATIVES ON THE BRINK OF EXTINCTION

TO SHOP ALONE OR TO SHOP WITH HIM

(WHEN TO KNOW IF HE'S A HANDICAP)

FIRST-TIME PARENTHOOD: UNBEARABLE BEHAVIOR EXPOSED

SIGNS THAT YOU'RE IN LOVE (OR OVER-CAFFEINATED)

EFFECTIVE BIRTH CONTROL

TELL ME HOW OLD YOU ARE, AND I'LL TELL YOU WHAT YOU EXPECT FROM A MAN

TRUE OR FALSE?

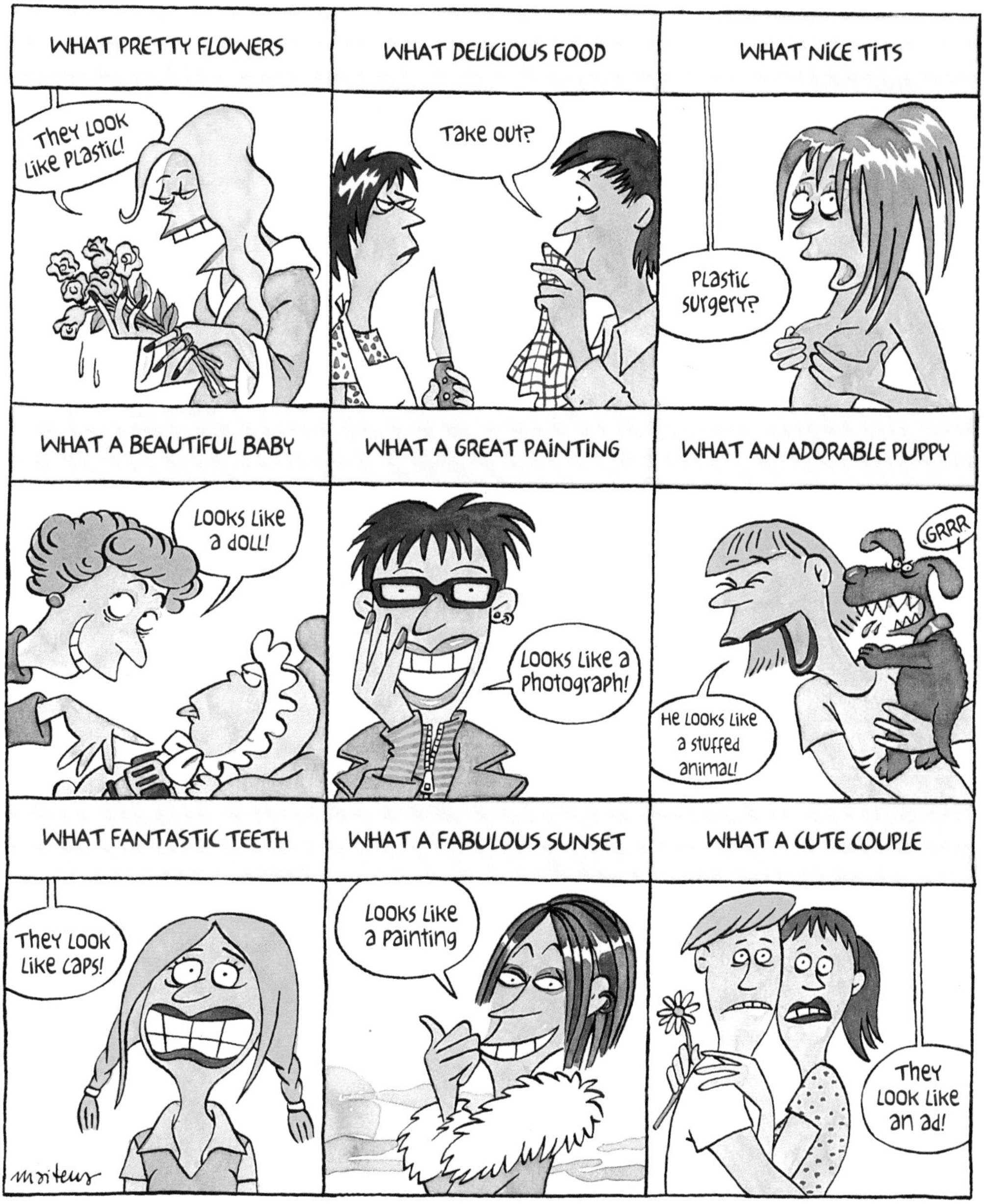

BROWN BAG REQUESTS

SUPERMARKET PERILS

WARNING: WHEN WEARING PLATFORMS . . .

SIX NASTY THINGS TO STEP ON

BEWARE OF SYNONYMS!

BETTER TO BE ALONE THAN IN BAD COMPANY

WHEN YOU'RE SINGLE, YOU HAVE SO MUCH TIME ON YOUR HANDS THAT YOU'RE JUST DYING TO TAKE CARE OF A MAN

WHEN YOU HAVE A MAN, YOU NEVER HAVE ANY TIME TO TAKE CARE OF YOURSELF

Honeeeey...

WHEN YOU'RE SINGLE, YOU HAVE TONS OF THINGS YOU WOULD LIKE TO TELL SOMEONE

Dear diary...

WHEN YOU HAVE A MAN, YOU HAVE NOTHING TO SAY TO HIM

WHEN YOU'RE SINGLE, YOU TAKE ALL THE TIME IN THE WORLD TO GET READY

WHEN YOU HAVE A MAN, YOU DON'T EVEN HAVE TIME TO PUT ON LIPSTICK

Come on!

WHEN YOU'RE SINGLE, YOU GO FOR A WAXING EVERY TWENTY DAYS

WHEN YOU HAVE A MAN, YOU SHAVE EVERY FOUR MONTHS

WHEN YOU'RE SINGLE, YOU'RE IN TOUCH WITH ALL YOUR FRIENDS

WHEN YOU HAVE A MAN, YOU DON'T EVEN CALL YOUR MOTHER

RING!! RING!! RING!!

WHEN YOU'RE SINGLE, IT SEEMS A WASTE THAT A GIRL LIKE YOU DOESN'T HAVE A BOYFRIEND

WHEN YOU HAVE A MAN, YOU CAN'T UNDERSTAND WHAT HE SEES IN YOU

A WOMAN IN LOVE AND OTHER STRANGE BEHAVIOR

RUN, DON'T WALK, AWAY FROM THESE MEN

THE VIRTUAL REALITY OF LOVE

LOVE IS BLIND

AND SOMETIMES DEAF . . .

. . . AND ALSO DUMB

DON'T FOLLOW FASHION, SET IT!

RIDICULOUS THINGS RIDICULOUS WOMEN TELL THEMSELVES

THINGS COUPLES DISCOVER WHEN BUILDING A HOUSE

IN SICKNESS AND IN HEALTH

DIFFICULT THINGS TO SAY TO DIFFICULT PEOPLE

HEALTH NUTS

THINGS THAT TAKE YOU TO THE EDGE!

COMMANDMENTS FOR THE PERFECT FAMILY

WHAT USED TO BE SHOCKING IS NOW DEMURE

GOOD REASONS TO NOT HELP YOUR CHILD
WITH HOMEWORK

TELL ME YOUR AGE, AND I'LL TELL YOU YOUR HAIR COLOR

DESPERATELY SEEKING "THE ONE"

THE FIRST SIX THINGS YOU FEEL FOR YOUR EX

TELL ME YOUR BODY TYPE
AND I'LL TELL YOU WHAT ANIMAL YOU LOOK LIKE

WHO SAID THE GOOD OLD DAYS WERE BETTER?

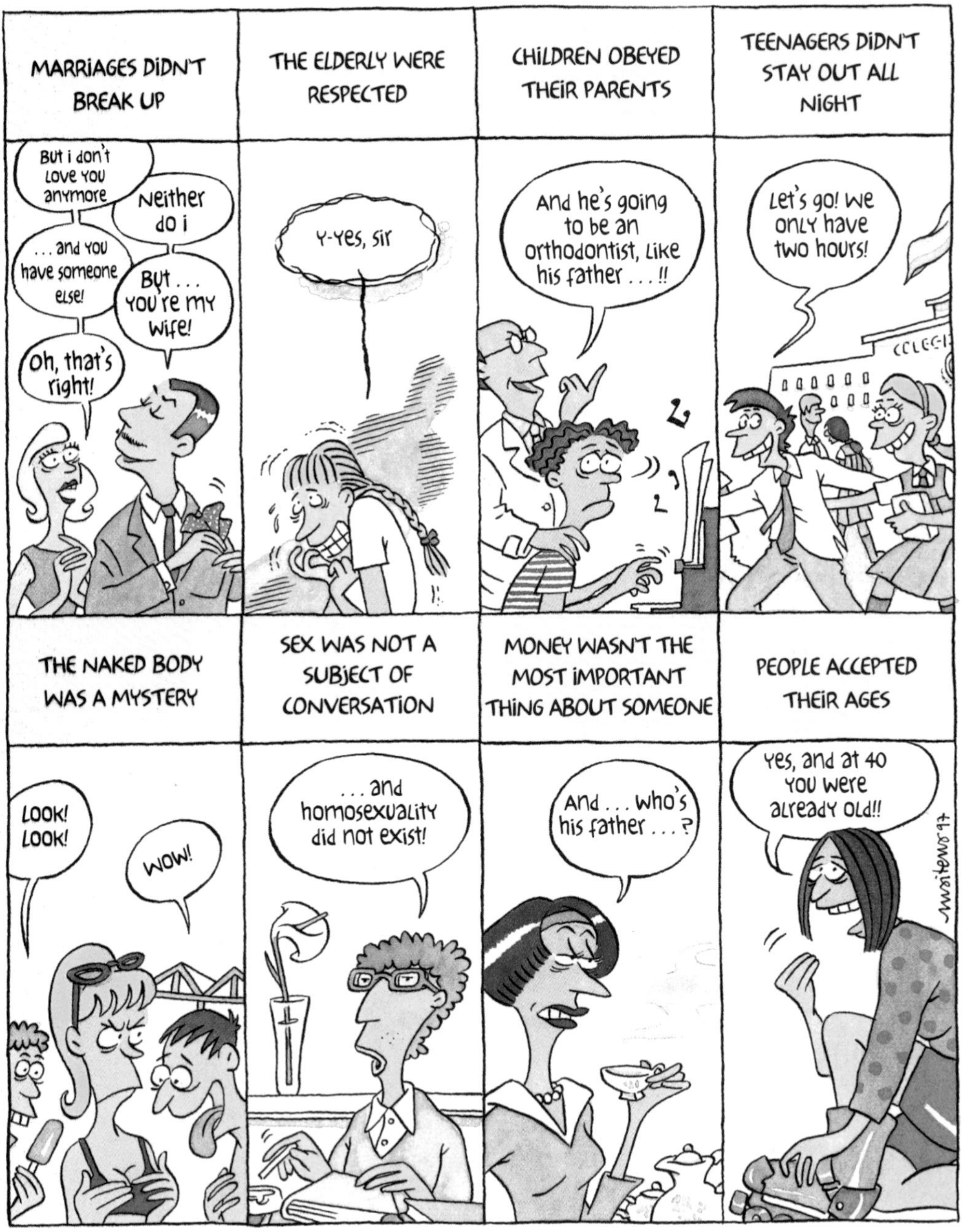

THOSE CUTE IDEAS THAT CHILDREN HAVE

WHEN YOU'RE LEFT TALKING TO YOURSELF

REFLECTIONS ON THE SUBJECT OF BOOBS

A WOMAN CAN FIND FAULT WITH ANYTHING

THE WEATHER IS GREAT FOR STROLLING OUTDOORS . . .

Oh Yeah? in this outfit?

THE AFTERNOONS ARE PERFECT FOR SUNBATHING . . .

Yeah, right! With this belly!

. . . ON WARM EVENINGS YOU CAN DRINK COLD BEER.

Sure? With who, huh?

huh?!?

VACATION TIME IS COMING UP. . .

Ha!

With what money?

THE YEAR IS ALMOST OVER!

Already?

Another one, gone?

BEST OF ALL, THE HOLIDAYS ARE ALMOST HERE!!

WAAAAH!!

maitena 97

HARDLY ECSTATIC THOUGHTS ON AESTHETICS

SPRING FASHION 2005
THE REVELATIONS OF REVEALING CLOTHING

BEAUTY IS DARING OR JUST PLAIN DEMENTED

THE FOUR SEASONS

THINGS YOU ONLY NOTICE ONCE THEY'VE HAPPENED TO YOU

MOTHER-DAUGHTER RELATIONSHIPS,
THAT MARVELOUS UNCONDITIONAL LOVE

THE EVOLUTION OF THE MOTHER-DAUGHTER BOND

WOMEN AND THEIR RELATIONSHIP WITH COMPLIMENTS

WHY WOMEN HATE ASKING THEIR FAMILY, "WHAT DO YOU WANT TO EAT?"

SIX THINGS TO REMEMBER WHEN YOUR SWEETHEART GOES OUT OF TOWN AND YOU'RE LEFT ON YOUR OWN

WHERE DID OUR WONDERFUL CHILDREN PICK UP THOSE DREADFUL HABITS?

SIX IRREFUTABLE CLUES THAT YOUR BOYFRIEND IS REPLACING YOUR DAD

ROADS THAT LEAD A WOMAN NOWHERE

TYPICAL MISUNDERSTANDINGS

THREE THINGS TO REMEMBER ABOUT THAT "FIRST TIME"

THREE GOOD THOUGHTS WHEN FACING THAT PERIOD WHEN YOU HAVE NO PERIOD!

KIDS AND SEX: TO HAVE OR HAVE NOT?

FILMS THAT DON'T GET A MAN IN THE MOOD

THREE GOOD QUESTIONS TO BREAK UP THE ROUTINE

WHAT A LOVER IS FOR

THE FEMALE FIXATION ON ANNIVERSARIES!

TYPICAL SOUVENIRS A FAMILY BRINGS BACK
FROM THEIR VACATION

WINTER VACATION IS HERE!

MEMORABLE MOMENTS A DIVORCED MOM HAS BEFORE LEAVING ON A TRIP WITH HER CHILDREN

POSSIBLE REASONS WHY A MAN DOESN'T TALK

MEN CAN NEVER FIND ANYTHING!

TELL ME HOW OLD YOU ARE,
AND I'LL TELL YOU WHAT'S IN YOUR PURSE

10 YEARS OLD

- Elastic bands and bobby pins
- Gum
- Barbie diary
- Glow-in-the-dark comb
- Boy-band photos
- One dollar
- Keys to diary and bike lock
- Panda bear

20 YEARS OLD

- Sunglasses with color lenses
- Condoms
- Address book
- Brush and blush
- Boyfriend's photo
- Cash
- House keys
- Three CDs

30 YEARS OLD

- Sunglasses
- Artificial sweetener
- A Palm Pilot
- Makeup bag
- Your baby's photo
- ATM card & credit card
- House and car keys
- Pacifier and disposable diapers

40 YEARS OLD

- Sunglasses and reading glasses
- Herbal supplements
- Cellular phone
- Tweezers and nail file
- Baby's same old photo
- ATM card & 4 credit cards
- Keys to house, car and office
- Extra pair of pantyhose

50 YEARS OLD

- Two pairs of glasses (reading and distance)
- Valium, Prozac or equivalent
- Self-help book
- Perfume
- Three old I.D. photos
- ATM card & 4 credit cards plus checkbook
- House and car keys plus country-house keys
- A Godiva chocolate bar

OVER 60 YEARS OLD

- Two pairs of bifocals
- A small drugstore
- City map
- Rain cap
- Grandchildren's photos
- Change purse
- House keys, including your kids' houses
- A bag with Tupperware

maitena

FALL-WINTER COLLECTIONS—
THE BIG THING THIS SEASON IS A LAID-BACK APPROACH . . .

MORE FALL-WINTER COLLECTIONS:
START SHAKING 'CAUSE THIS IS WHAT YOU'LL BE WEARING!

HOW HE GOES TO BED WILL TELL YOU WHAT KIND OF RELATIONSHIP TO EXPECT!

TELL ME YOUR AGE, AND I'LL TELL YOU
WHO YOU MET BY SURPRISE ON VACATION . . .

THOSE UNFORGETTABLE MOMENTS ON CHRISTMAS EVE

GOING TO A RESTAURANT TO CELEBRATE

THINGS ONLY WOMEN CAN GIVE UP!

WHAT WE'VE BEEN ACCUSED OF THROUGH THE DECADES

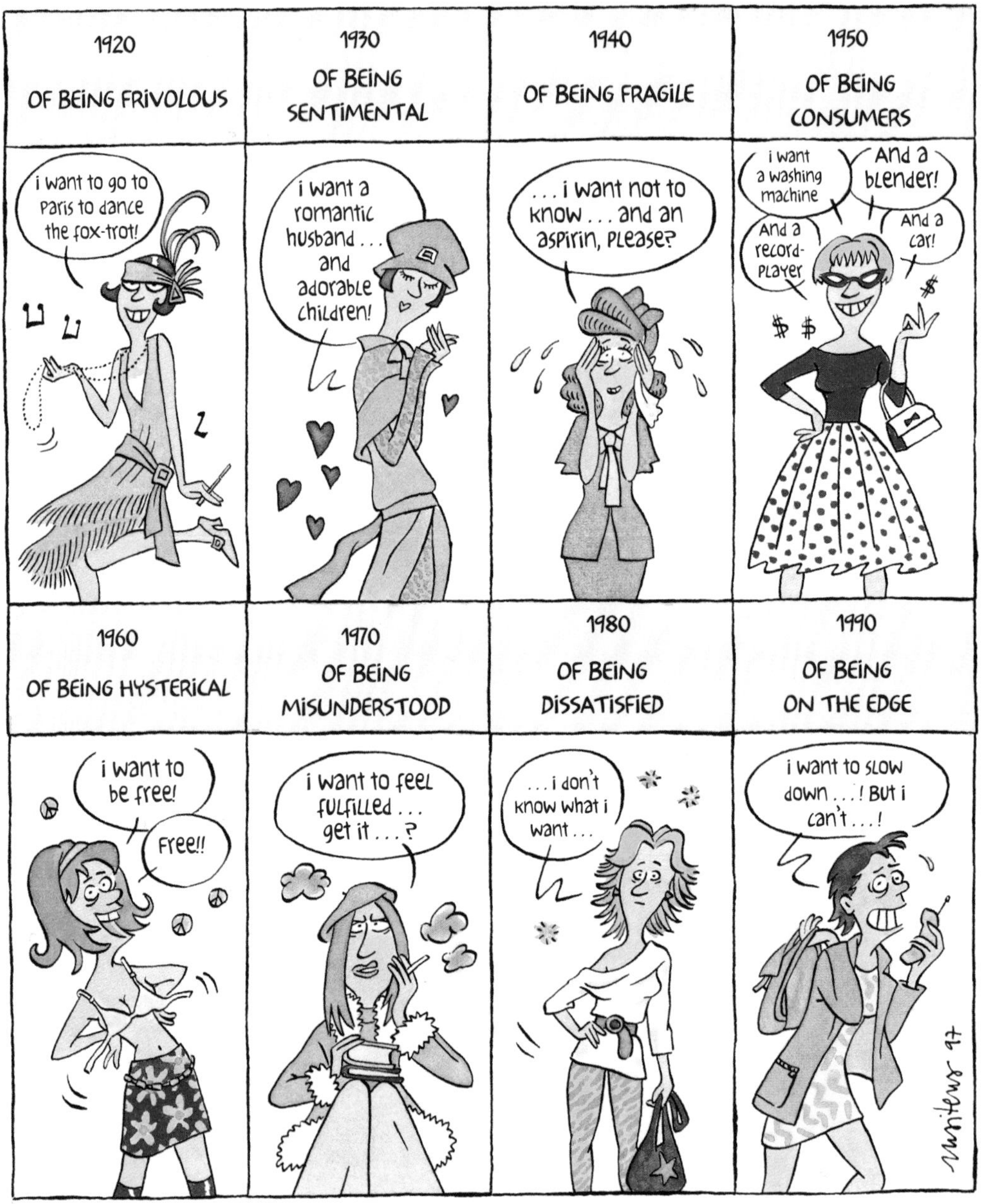

ABOUT MAITENA

I WAS BORN IN 1962, I THINK. BECAUSE I WAS THE SIXTH OF SEVEN SIBLINGS AND MY MOM HAD LITTLE TIME TO REMEMBER INSIGNIFICANT DETAILS.

COME ON, MARI... LOLI... ANI... CARLI... RAM... PA ...

MAITENA

FROM EARLY CHILDHOOD, I TRIED TO LEAD A NORMAL LIFE.

...BUT I WAS NO GOOD AT SPORTS, I FOUND SCHOOL BORING

AND I WAS TOO MUCH OF A FEMINIST TO BECOME A HOUSEMAKER

SO, I BEGAN DRAWING TO KEEP MYSELF BUSY. AT MY HOUSE, IF YOU DIDN'T KEEP BUSY, THERE WAS ALWAYS A CHORE WAITING FOR YOU.

...SO, THAT'S HOW I DISCOVERED, THAT WHILE I WAS DRAWING, MY THOUGHTS COULD ROAM FREE, WITHOUT ANYONE ATTEMPTING TO EDUCATE ME.

SO MUCH THINKING MADE ME REALIZE THAT, IF EVER I MARRIED, I WOULD NEVER BE AN INDEPENDENT WOMAN.

I WAS ONLY 17 AND WAS ALREADY BEING PUBLISHED IN THOSE WAITING-ROOM MAGAZINES!

STILL I GOT MARRIED, BECAUSE HE UNDERSTOOD MY JOKES.

(UNFORTUNATELY THAT WAS ALL HE UNDERSTOOD)

BY 19, I ALREADY HAD TWO WONDERFUL KIDS, THREE LOUSY JOBS, ALL SORT OF PROBLEMS...

AND GRAY HAIR!

I SEPARATED AT 24

I WAS TOO YOUNG FOR THAT MUCH RESPONSIBILITY

I DECIDED MY LIFE LACKED SOME SEX, DRUGS AND ROCK'N'ROLL

I DON'T REMEMBER MUCH ABOUT THE NEXT FEW YEARS

BUT I USED RED HENNA IN MY HAIR

MY DRAWINGS BEGAN TO SHOW UP IN RACY MAGAZINES IN THE FORM OF EROTIC COMICS. I ALSO ILLUSTRATED CHILDREN'S BOOKS I LIVED IN FEAR OF DELIVERING THE WRONG ENVELOPE.

- BUT THIS IS NOT COLUMBUS ABOUT TO SAIL FROM SPAIN!!

EVENTUALLY, IN 1992, WHEN I WAS JUST READY TO DO SOMETHING ELSE, FED UP BY THE FACT THAT NOBODY SEEMED INTERESTED IN MY WORK, A VERY IMPORTANT MAGAZINE CALLED ME UP ASKING FOR A COMIC STRIP PAGE. IT WAS A SUCCESS. THE ENTIRE EDITING DEPARTMENT WAS IN TEARS...

WOMEN ON THE EDGE!

...SO I BECAME WHAT I'D ALWAYS WANTED TO BE...

A BLONDE

TIRED OF DESPERATELY LOOKING FOR LOVE, AND ABOUT TO BECOME A LESBIAN, I MET THE MAN OF MY LIFE

ONE HITCH: HE WAS DATING A FRIEND OF MINE

I LOST A FRIEND

LOVE MADE ME A HAPPY WOMAN. AT 37, TWENTY YEARS AFTER MY FIRST CHILD, I GAVE BIRTH TO MY THIRD, AND THOUGH MY SELF-ESTEEM GREW WITHOUT RESTRAINT AND TODAY MY HUMOR TRAVELS AROUND THE WORLD, THERE'S STILL SOMETHING I FAIL TO UNDERSTAND...

HOW, IN THE END, EVERYTHING TURNED OUT SO WELL

- HANDSOME!
- SENSITIVE!
- INTELLIGENT!
- FUNNY!
- WEALTHY!
- AND MY AGE!

maitena